THE REAL
Wolfgang Amadeus Mozart

45th Parallel Press

Published in the United States of America by Cherry Lake Publishing
Ann Arbor, Michigan
www.cherrylakepublishing.com

Reading Adviser: Marla Conn MS, Ed., Literacy specialist, Read-Ability, Inc.
Book Cover Design: Felicia Macheske

Photo Credits: © Elnur/Shutterstock.com, Cover, 1; © Everett Historical/Shutterstock.com, 5, 27;
© vasiliki/iStock, 7; © ilbusca/iStock, 9, 17; © Library of Congress/Reproduction No. LC-DIG-pga-01250, 11;
© Morphart Creation/Shutterstock.com, 12; © The Hunterian, University of Glasgow 2018, 15; © Olesya
Nickolaeva/Shutterstock.com, 19; © Soru Epotok/Shutterstock.com, 20; © Marcel Derweduwen/
Shutterstock.com, 23; © Marzolino/Shutterstock.com, 24; © NaxosUSA/Shutterstock.com, 29;
© Library of Congress/Reproduction No. LC-DIG-det-4a27867, 30

Graphic Elements Throughout: © iulias/Shutterstock.com; © Thinglass/Shutterstock.com; © kzww/
Shutterstock.com; © A_Lesik/Shutterstock.com; © MegaShabanov/Shutterstock.com; © Groundback
Atelier/Shutterstock.com; © saki80/Shutterstock.com

45th Parallel Press is an imprint of Cherry Lake Publishing.

Library of Congress Cataloging-in-Publication Data

Names: Loh-Hagan, Virginia, author.
Title: The real Wolfgang Amadeus Mozart / by Virginia Loh-Hagan.
Description: Ann Arbor, Michigan : Cherry Lake Publishing, [2019] | Series: History Uncut |
    Includes bibliographical references and index.
Identifiers: LCCN 2018035190 | ISBN 9781534143357 (hardcover) | ISBN 9781534141117 (pdf) |
    ISBN 9781534139916 (pbk.) | ISBN 9781534142312 (hosted ebook)
Subjects: LCSH: Mozart, Wolfgang Amadeus, 1756-1791—Juvenile literature. |
    Composers—Austria—Biography—Juvenile literature.
Classification: LCC ML3930.M9 L65 2019 | DDC 780.92 [B]—dc23
LC record available at https://lccn.loc.gov/2018035190

Cherry Lake Publishing would like to acknowledge the work of The Partnership for 21st Century Skills.
Please visit www.p21.org for more information.

Printed in the United States of America
Corporate Graphics

Table of Contents

Chapter 1
Wolfgang Amadeus Mozart
The Story You Know 4

Chapter 2
A Musical Miracle 6

Chapter 3
Like Sister, Like Brother 10

Chapter 4
Sister Love 14

Chapter 5
Musical Pets 18

Chapter 6
Toilet Humor 22

Chapter 7
Losing It 26

Timeline 30

Consider This! 31
Learn More 31
Glossary 32
Index 32
About the Author 32

Wolfgang Amadeus Mozart
The Story You Know

Wolfgang Amadeus Mozart was a famous composer. Composers are people who write music.

He was a child prodigy. A prodigy is someone with amazing skills or talents. Mozart played piano and violin at an early age. He started composing at age 5. He performed in front of kings and queens. By age 17, he had composed over 600 songs. He helped develop classical music. Classical music includes symphonies, concertos, operas, and sonatas. These are special musical forms.

Mozart's work inspired many people. His music is played all the time. But there's more to his story ...

Mozart didn't like trumpets.

CHAPTER 2

A Musical Miracle

Mozart's birth name is interesting. It's Johannes
Chrysostomus Wolfgangus Theophilus Mozart.
"Johannes" is like John. "Wolfgang" is a German male
name. It means wolf's path. It's the name of Mozart's
grandfather. "Chrysostomus" means golden mouth.
"Theophilus" is Greek. It means loved by God.
It's the name of Mozart's godfather. Mozart preferred
"Amadeus." "Amadeus" is the Latin form of "Theophilus."

Mozart was born on January 27, 1756. January 27
was the feast day of **Saint** John Chrysostom. Saints
are holy people. Mozart's first two names were in
honor of this saint.

Mozart was playful. He sometimes signed his name as "Wolfgangus Amadeus Mozartus."

1756

> The Seven Years' War was the first world war. It's called World War Zero. It affected Europe, America, West Africa, India, and the Philippines. There were two main sides. One side was led by Great Britain. Another side was led by France. The main issue was about land. There were battles. Towns were burned down.

> Many people died in the Black Hole of Calcutta on June 20, 1756. Calcutta is in India. The Black Hole was a jail. It was 18 feet (5.5 meters) long. It was 14 feet (4.3 m) wide. It had two small windows. It was hot. It was cramped. Many British soldiers were taken to the Black Hole. They were prisoners of war. They were given little water. They were abused by the guards. Few people survived.

> The Catherine Palace was completed. It's in St. Petersburg, Russia. It's the summer home of Russian leaders. It's over 1,000 feet (305 m) long. It's made of over 220 pounds (100 kilograms) of gold.

"I am, I was, I have been, oh! That I were, would to heavens I were! I will or shall be, would, could, or should be—what?—A blockhead!" — Wolfgang Amadeus Mozart

Mozart could speak several languages. He liked to play with his name. He changed his middle name to other language forms. Starting in 1770, he called himself "Amadeo" or "Amadè." In some cases, his middle name is listed as "Adam." At a concert in Prague, his middle name was "Gottlieb." "Gottlieb" means God's love.

Anagrams are word puzzles. By changing around the letters of words, people can form new words. "Wolfgang Amadeus Mozart" is an anagram of "a famous German waltz god."

Mozart signed his wedding papers as "Wolfgang Amadè Mozart."

CHAPTER 3

Like Sister, Like Brother

Leopold and Anna Maria were Mozart's parents. They had seven children. Only two lived. The oldest child was Maria Anna. She was called Nannerl. Mozart was the youngest child.

Both Nannerl and Mozart were musically gifted. At age 7, Leopold gave Nannerl piano lessons. Mozart was 3 years old. He looked up to his sister. He copied her. He played notes on the piano. Then he started playing. By 1762, Nannerl and Mozart were really good. They were ready to perform in public. They did the Mozart family grand tour. Many people came to see them. They were impressed by the young prodigies.

Mozart played songs. His father wrote them down.

Nannerl and Mozart were very close. They created a secret language. They created a fantasy world. The world was called Kingdom of Back. Nannerl and Mozart were the king and queen.

Nannerl was just as good as Mozart. Some people thought she was better. Leopold said, "My little girl, although she is only 12 years old, is one of the most skillful players in Europe." Mozart said, "My dear sister! I am in awe that you can compose so well. In a word, the song you wrote is beautiful."

But Nannerl was female. Women couldn't perform in public as adults. Nannerl stopped touring. Mozart became the star.

Some people think Nannerl helped Mozart write some of his songs.

All in the Family

Leopold Mozart was Mozart's father. He was born in 1719. He was a violinist. He was a composer. He was a teacher. His most famous student was his son. Leopold became a violinist for the Austrian prince. He became a court composer. He wrote a famous book about teaching violin. He showed off his children. He took them to many different cities. People judged him for this. They thought he was using his children to make money and gain fame for himself. Leopold thought it was his duty to develop his children's talents. He also thought it was his duty to show off their talents to the world. Leopold's father wanted him to become a priest. But Leopold didn't want that. He wanted to be a musician. He was more famous for teaching than performing. Leopold raised his daughter's son. His daughter named her son Leopold.

"Love, love, love—that is the soul of genius."
— Wolfgang Amadeus Mozart

CHAPTER 4

Sister Love

The Mozarts weren't the only musical family in town. The Weber family was also musical. There were four sisters. They were all singers.

In 1777, Mozart went to Germany. He became Aloysia Weber's singing teacher. He fell in love with her. He wanted to marry her. Aloysia rejected him. Mozart left. He went to Paris to find work. Aloysia married an actor.

The father of the Weber family died in 1782. The mother rented their house. She needed to make money. Mozart returned to Germany. He stayed at the Weber house. He fell in love with another Weber girl.

Constanze was a good partner. She was down-to-earth.

THAT Happened?!?

Satoyuki Fujimura is from Japan. He earned a world record. He did the most finger snaps in a minute. He can do 296 clicks in 60 seconds. He pushed his body to the limit to do this. He did this on Japanese television. He did it in front of many people. He did it in front of an official judge. The judge was Kaoru Ishikawa. Ishikawa timed Fujimura for a minute. Then, he watched the recording. He watched in slow motion. There were two professional sound engineers there. They all counted the clicks. Only snaps made with the thumb and middle finger counted. Fujimura learned to snap from his mother. Fujimura made a video. He showed off his skills. He finger snapped to Mozart's "Rondo alla Turca." This piece is also known as the "Turkish March." It's fast. Mozart wrote this around age 27.

"I pay no attention whatever to anybody's praise or blame. I simply follow my own feelings."
—Wolfgang Amadeus Mozart

He asked Constanze to marry him. But his father didn't approve. Mozart married her anyway. They had six children. Only two lived. Their names were Karl Thomas and Franz Xaver Wolfgang.

Mozart loved Constanze. He wrote, "Without my Constanze, I cannot be happy and merry." He wrote her many love letters. He wrote, "I am forever your Mozart who loves you with his entire soul."

He helped the Weber girls. He wrote songs for them to sing. He wrote an opera. The main **heroine** was named Constanze. Heroines are female heroes.

Mozart sang in public until he was 13 years old.

CHAPTER 5

Musical Pets

Mozart loved nature. He loved animals. He had several pets. At age 14, he had a pet **canary**. Canaries are songbirds. He wrote a letter to his sister Nannerl. He asked, "Write me. How is Mr. Canary? Does he still sing?"

Mozart had a pet dog. The dog's name was Miss Bimbes. The dog was also called Bimperl or Pimperl. Mozart **dedicated** one of his songs to the dog. Dedicate means to write or perform something for someone as a compliment or to show appreciation. Mozart wrote to Nannerl again when he was 17. He asked, "How is Miss Bimbes? Please present all manner of **compliments** to her." Compliments are good thoughts.

Mozart sold his horse. He didn't like riding horses.

Mozart seemed to like his pet **starling** best. Starlings are songbirds. Mozart bought the starling in 1784. He had it for 3 years. He wrote about it in his journal. He wrote down tunes sung by the starling. He taught it to sing the opening theme of one of his piano concertos.

The starling died a week after his father died. Mozart couldn't go to his father's funeral. He was too far away. So, he planned a big funeral for the starling. He buried it in his garden. He wrote a poem. The poem starts, "Here rests a bird called Starling. A foolish little Darling."

Mozart wrote a piece called *A Musical Joke*.
It copies a starling's noisy singing.

Bad Blood

Antonio Salieri lived from 1750 to 1825. He was an Italian musician. He's famous for developing opera. He moved to Austria at age 16. The Hapsburgs ruled Austria. They hired Salieri as the music director. Salieri had this job for over 30 years. He taught Liszt, Schubert, and Beethoven. Many people think Salieri and Mozart were enemies. They think Salieri was jealous of Mozart. Salieri was older. Mozart was getting a lot of attention. Some people think Salieri poisoned Mozart to death. Others think Mozart was jealous of Salieri. They both applied to be Princess Elisabeth's music teacher. She was the princess of Württemberg in Austria. The princess chose Salieri. Salieri had more important jobs than Mozart. This made Mozart mad. In 1781, he wrote to his father. He wrote, "The only one who counts in [the emperor's] eyes is Salieri." Mozart didn't like how Italians were in Austrian courts. He blamed Salieri for not having more success in Vienna.

"You should show the whole world that you are not afraid. Be silent, if you choose. But, when it is necessary, speak. And, speak in such a way that people will remember it." — Wolfgang Amadeus Mozart

CHAPTER 6

Toilet Humor

Mozart was very playful. He had a good sense of **humor**. Humor means fun. Mozart especially loved poop jokes.

He wrote many letters. He wrote to his friends and family. Many of his letters had poop jokes. Most of his poop jokes were sent to his father, mother, sister, and cousin. Leopold, Anna Maria, and Nannerl would also write poop jokes back to Mozart.

In 1777, he wrote to his cousin. He wrote a poop poem. The poem started, "Well, I wish you good night. But first, poop in your bed. And make it burst."

The fancy name for poop jokes is scatological humor.

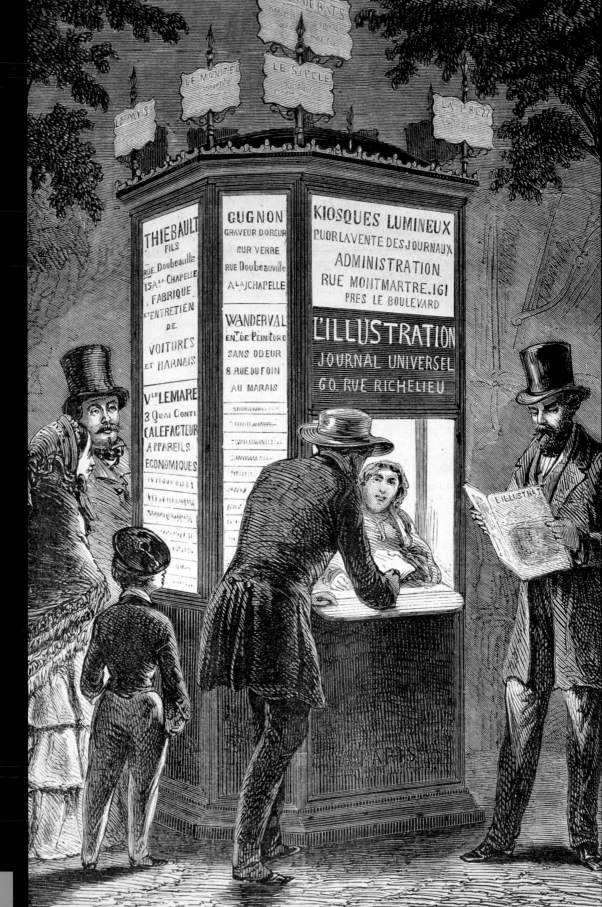

Mozart also wrote songs about poop. Some people think he wrote poop songs to Aloysia. He was mad at her for rejecting him.

Most of his poop songs were for fun. He mainly wrote them at parties. He wrote them to entertain his friends.

Not all his jokes had poop. He wrote *A Musical Joke*. He wrote in mistakes. This song makes fun of bad musicians. It also makes fun of snobs who stick too closely to musical forms.

Mozart also wrote riddles and anagrams. He published some in newspapers.

CHAPTER 7

Losing It

Mozart spent a lot of money. He liked fancy things. He liked to party. At the end of his life, Mozart was poor. He was in **debt**. Debt means owing money. Mozart was also sick. Many people thought he was losing his mind.

In 1791, Mozart was hired to write a **requiem**. Requiems are songs for dead people. Mozart needed the money. He didn't know who hired him. He thought it was Death itself. He thought the requiem was for his own death. This scared him. It made him very sad. His mind was playing tricks on him.

Mozart got really sick in November. Constanze and one of her sisters took care of him. Mozart died on December 5, 1791. No one knows how he died.

Mozart wrote many songs in his last year. His most famous work was the opera called *The Magic Flute*.

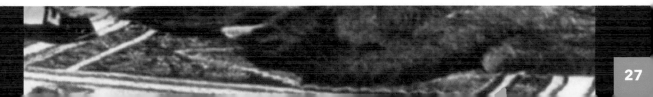

Explained by
SCIENCE

Some people think Mozart was left-handed. Only about 10 percent of people are left-handed. Scientists think that being left-handed is determined by gene activity. Genes are cells that determine people's character traits. This activity happens in the spinal cord. Spines are backbones. The motor cortex is a part of the brain. It controls arm and hand movements. It sends a message to the spinal cord. This becomes a movement. Being left-handed is determined when babies are in wombs. It's determined in the 8th week. Babies suck their left or right thumbs in week 13. Until week 15, the motor cortex and the spinal cord aren't connected yet. Babies choose a favorite hand before the brain controls the body.

"If only the whole world could feel the power of harmony." – Wolfgang Amadeus Mozart

There are many possible causes. Some examples are sickness, poison, and head injury.

Mozart didn't finish the requiem. Someone else finished it for him. The song was played at his funeral.

Mozart died without any money. He was buried in a **common** grave. Common means not of royal blood. Common graves were graves in the ground. They could be dug up after a few years. This was because graveyards needed more space. Royal graves couldn't be dug up. These graves were in a **vault**. A vault is a protected space. Nobody knows what happened to Mozart's bones. But his music will live on forever.

Mozart's requiem was also played at the funeral of Frederic Chopin. He was a composer who died in 1849.

Timeline

1756: Mozart was born. He was born in Salzburg, Austria.

1761: Mozart gave his first public performance. He played the piano.

1762: Mozart and his sister went to Munich and Vienna. They performed for the court. Their father showed them off as prodigies.

1763: Mozart and his sister performed in many European cities. They performed in Paris and London. Mozart began to compose.

1764: Mozart wrote his first symphony.

1768: Mozart wrote his first opera. It's *La Finta Simplice*. He also wrote a mass.

1770: Mozart visited Italy for the first time. He heard a song in the Sistine Chapel. It's a hard song. It has five different parts. Mozart wrote down the song from memory.

1772: Mozart was hired as a concertmaster. This means he was the leader of the violins. He had to live in Salzburg.

1777: Mozart became tired of Salzburg. He went on a long trip with his mother. He met Aloysia Weber.

1778: Mozart went to Paris. He composed ballet music. His mother died.

1779: Mozart moved back to Salzburg.

1781–1782: Mozart moved to the Weber family's home in Munich, Germany. He fell in love with Constanze Weber. They married and moved to Vienna.

1786: Mozart traveled to Prague. He saw the premiere of two of his operas.

1787: Mozart met Beethoven. Mozart's father died.

1791: Mozart played his last public concert. He died in early December.

Consider This!

Take a Position! Learn more about the "Mozart effect." This is the idea that people are smarter after listening to classical music. Do you agree or disagree? Argue your point with reasons and evidence.

Say What? Mozart was a child prodigy. Research three other child prodigies. Explain what makes them special. Explain what they have in common. Explain how they're different.

Think About It! Listen to Mozart's music. Did you like it? Why or why not? How did it make you feel? What makes Mozart a "master of melody"?

Learn More

Krull, Kathleen, and Kathryn Hewitt (illustr.). *Lives of the Musicians: Good Times, Bad Times (and What the Neighbors Thought)*. San Diego: Harcourt, 2002.

McDonough, Yona Zeldis. *Who Was Wolfgang Amadeus Mozart?* New York: Grosset & Dunlap, 2003.

Weeks, Marcus. *Mozart: The Boy Who Changed the World With His Music*. Washington, DC: National Geographic, 2013.

anagrams (AN-uh-grams) word puzzles in which people change around the letters of words to form new words

canary (kuh-NAIR-ee) songbird

classical (KLAS-ih-kuhl) type of music developed between 1750 and 1820 that includes symphonies, concertos, operas, and sonatas

common (KAH-muhn) not of royal blood

compliments (KAHM-pluh-muhnts) good thoughts, nice comments

composer (kuhm-POH-zur) someone who writes music

debt (DET) the owing of money

dedicated (DED-ih-kate-id) wrote or performed something for someone as a compliment or to show appreciation

heroine (HER-oh-in) female hero

humor (HYOO-mur) fun, amusement, quality of being funny

prodigy (PRAH-dih-jee) a person with extraordinary skills or talent

requiem (REK-wee-uhm) a song for dead people

saint (SAYNT) a holy person

starling (STAHR-ling) songbird

vault (VAWLT) a burial chamber

Index

classical music, 4

finger snaps, 16

left-handedness, 28

Magic Flute, The, 27

Mozart, Leopold, 10, 11, 12, 13, 20

Mozart, Nannerl, 10, 12, 18

Mozart, Wolfgang Amadeus, 4

and Constanze Weber, 15, 17

family, 10
father, 10, 11, 12, 13, 20
illness and death, 26, 29
name, 6, 7, 9
pets, 18–20
as prodigy, 4, 10
and Salieri, 21
sense of humor, 22–25
sister, 10, 12, 18

timeline, 30
and Weber sisters, 14–15, 17

requiems, 26, 29

Salieri, Antonio, 21

Weber sisters, 14–15, 1

About the Author

Dr. Virginia Loh-Hagan is an author, university professor, and former classroom teacher. She loves playing Mozart songs on her piano. She visited Mozart's home in Salzburg, Austria. She lives in San Diego with her very tall husband and very naughty dogs. To learn more about her, visit www.virginialoh.com.